POEMS You&I

POEMS
You & I

Ralph de Toledano

PELICAN PUBLISHING COMPANY

GRETNA 1978

Library of Congress Cataloging in Publication Data

De Toledano, Ralph, 1916—
   Poems, you & I.

   I. Title. II. Title: You & I.
PS3554.E85P6   811'.5'4   77-17944
ISBN 0-88289-173-1

Manufactured in the United States of America

Published by Pelican Publishing Company, Inc.
630 Burmaster Street, Gretna, Louisiana 70053

To
ZARITA NAHON
dear aunt, dear friend
whose life has been her poetry

POEMS You&I

I

I write of "you"—
women who have circled my bed
or commerced
with my heart.
Each of you lives
within the tissue
that contains me.
You make a fine *ménage*
of *döppelgangers*
to frighten
each new arrival.

II

Flowers on the table,
picked by you.
Framed by the window,
forsythia yellow in the sun.
A cardinal in a branch
addressing the morning.
You, tidy in a blue
housecoat, hair combed.
Coffee and bacon
calling from the kitchen.
The touch of fingers
thanking the day.

III

We came on a course of water,
less than a stream, more than a brook,
and watched it happily
as if its little depth were magic.
The water made no sound
but returned the sun's color
and ran for darkness in the overhang
of trees and jutting boulders.
We watched it as long as we could,
then we went away.

IV

"Tell me," you said, hoping I'd speak
the quick disorder of my mind.
You sat before me head a-tilt,
face a plane of steel. "Tell me,"
you said. "You saw him die,
flexing the muscle of his life.
You saw death takes his eyes.
You were there but did not speak,
letting him die without the unction
of word or gesture." Time tumbled,
but we were engraved to the moment.
"You were no warmer than the slab
on which they laid him," you said,
your smile a razor on glass.
"You must have loved him very much—
you wore the sackcloth with such style,
though there was blood under your nails
and on your lashes." You circled me
as if I were a statue, encrusted, dredged
from the sea. "Tell me," you said,
but all the words that once
groped for deliverance had fled.

V

I touched you—do you remember?—
as if touching scorpions,
afraid that your answering touch
would turn them to little birds,
writhing flowers, anything
but what they were—and so it did
The little birds left wounds,
the flowers died,
and I miss the scorpions.

VI

There was a vixen
that knew each day
when I'd come by,
rifle in hand.
It sensed precisely
the accurate range
of those .22 calibres
and stayed beyond it,
laughing, I swear.
Once I was tempted
to bring a piece
whose longer arm
could reach across
to shatter that composure.
But a dead vixen
would have meant
nothing to me
and I'd have lost
the pleasure
of her company.

VII

We shared the same
small devils
that deny sleep
or jab fingernails
into nightmares.
Now the devils
are all mine.
I watch them
knowing where
they come from,
where they're going.

VIII

We could not know,
so empty was the plain,
that under earth
the little tigers lurked.
We saw the matted grass,
ahead the stunted shrubs,
dirt mounded and flattened,
unmarked by step or rut.
The sun should have warned us,
white in an untouched sky.
Without command we lurched
forward, wheels creaking.
And there we died.

IX

For many nights
the kitten slept
pressed to your face
and shoulder,
purring possession,
its nails ready
to make a protest
if you moved.
I'd wake, touching
its warmth and yours,
challenging the kinship.

X

I shouldn't have spoken,
and that applies to you.
Words are witches
with cackling power
to transmute suspicion
into hard fact.
Over a brew
of alcohol and tears
they slurp their incantations.
Now what am I to you
or you to me?
Two voices hung from a lamppost
with telephone wire.

XI

Waking, you did not know that the day
would end in screams and terror.
The room looked as it always looked,
its small appurtenances commonplace
as they had always been, the mirror
unsmashed, your clothing tossed about,
its disarray casual and comforting.
You touched yourself delighting
in the texture of your flesh, your hair,
and ate your breakfast with no concern
for ambushes in the teapot, mice in the milk.
The first cigarette was pleasant
to your mouth, its smoke a small incense.
You did not know—how could you know—
that hours away your blood would puddle,
that my tears would wet your face unnoticed.

XII

I've missed the falling snow
seen from a window
or felt on the face.
I've missed the cold
that sent me
to the shelter of your touch.
In the light that filtered
through the window
we saw ourselves in ways
alien to summer's heat.
Find me then when it's cold,
when a small flame
preserves the solstice,
guttering like a candle
that fails and brightens,
fails and grows.

XIII

The tides run cold in August
and spume rides the breakers
on overtreaded beaches.
Sand shows its impatience.
Fish bite avidly
and crabs fork out
in cancerous desires,
waiting for the coming flesh
in the murder of high water.

XIV

To say I love you
is to lay my shield
on the ground,
to leave myself
unarmed on a field
where many die
but few find resurrection.

XV

In spite of you
love came to its pleasance.
Your mouth derided it,
the shimmer of your eyes
blinked it away.
But it persisted,
purred like a cat
at its saucer.
It's all gone now—
rain fills
the footprints—
in spite of me
and what I said
to hold you.

XVI

Why in Amalfi did you call
or in Aleppo wink?
That's what you say happened
though I've not been there.
Not that it matters.
I'm simply someone
you've somewhere seen.
It might just as well
have been in Newark.

XVII

Walking in the woods,
did you ever find
a poisoned mushroom
and seeing it think,
"I could put this
in my pocket
against the day
when death is necessary"?
I'm sure you did
but then walked on.
Until it lifts the sheet
death is a whimsy.
But there was one
who stooped and picked,
reassured that destiny
was in his hand.

XVIII

I make my poems now
behind nailed shutters.
The words falter
and I dream of fields
bending to the wind.
But where's the sound
of thunder, the onetime
taste of flesh.
I tap on my pipe,
you tap on yours.
We are each other's
prisoner of war.

XIX

In Rome we stayed
at a new hotel
a short walk
from the Vatican.
But the Holy Father
was not well
and would not see us.
We drank *americanos,*
read *Daisy Miller,*
and roamed the Pincio.
In Madrid we found
the Prado too dark
to see the Grecos.
You hated the bullfights
and hated me
because I liked them.
The interview with Franco
died in the August heat—
he'd fled the city.
In Paris our hotel
had sagging beds
and sloping floors.
The wind was cold
off the Seine
but we stacked saucers
at sidewalk cafes
drinking *fine à l'eau.*
We had no appointments,
talked to no one.
At night you were
always tired
so we slept.

XX

You've measured it—
the road from here to there,
the heart's trajectory
in its dirty travel.
And I've measured you
while you were at your work.
Put down the tape.
The knife fits better
in your hand.

XXI

Driving back
on the broken highway
from Malaga to Estepona,
the dark was a wolf's mouth.
But we found the turning
and a whitewashed room.
The brandy was warm
in the glass, the bed hard,
and in our own darkness
the refuge we needed.

XXII

You pulled away
to look at my face,
searching for a sign
of some complicity.
But in your stare,
my eyes were gelatin
and my face melted.
Only your pain
brought me back.

XXIII

By this pale water legions stood
and watched the bivouac on the other side.
But now we are alone, you there.
I here, our wretched strength
caught in an eddy of the moon.
You wash socks in your helmet
sure I will not put rifle to shoulder
and squeeze death into your loins.
We're parted by just so many yards
of river, but there are screams
and small obscenities to save you.

XXIV

There was no time.
You raised the glass
I saw the bone
behind your eyes.
You drank
and it was gone.

XXV

The roll and welter of the waves
yellow the spume, flecked by tar.
The piper skips, probing for sand lice.
Terns revolve, guarding their young.
Jetsam is the trove, old bottles,
splintered wood, the wreck of picnics.
Yet here, feet planted in the swirl
of surf, salt drying on my face,
I once reached past the breakers
to rusty ships taking the tide.
Here I turned to hands that touched
my life, my hair—and here
I heard the voices, silent now.

XXVI

True, your goodbye
came as no surprise.
But you buried love
so quickly, I had no time
to answer, cry, or mourn.

XXVII

"I've done you in,"
you said. "I've caught
your soul, bottled it.
There's no escape for you."
Behind you I could see
the light evaporate.
We were so close
I heard the whisper
of your hair.
But you were dead,
stoppered like me.
Your voice was mine.

XXVIII

I took you by the hand
and led you to my room.
Our eyes were open.
Now desire lives on
but wanting is in the oven,
baked dry. The recipe
is lost, burned dead.

XXIX

"You bring so very little,
so very little," you said.
"The little easement
of love's temporary rash,
the tiny liberation.
Then it's into morning,
and what's the muster?
A little spasm, a big regret."
I never answer you.
Can I explain what cold
brings in the morning?
What I really mean
is that we're lost and found
but never redeemed.

XXX

The memory of love
was all you wanted.
You saved me for yesterday
and ate breakfast alone.

XXXI

Once in your anger
you said, "Lie to me."
My way of lying
was to tell the truth.
But there were times
when truth was more
than you or I could bear,
and so I lied.
Those lies still
live with us,
tattering flesh.
The question's there—
Amo, amas, amat?
But we'll never know.

XXXII

You've lost us, Donne!
Tears are not fashionable,
and who'd stand the sobbing,
the wit of deliberation?
We love in prose now.
No lutenist sounds
the call to bed.
He'd be wasting his time.
Before a chord was struck,
we'd have run the meter
between the sheets.
Today even rabbits
are more roundabout.
Love's tintinnabulation
comes four/four time,
not to your teasing measure.
We do not even joke
the way you did
in love's contemplation.
Yet there it is,
the fatal interview
of heart and marrow survives
the mutter of the traffic,
and pain is still the answer
now and tomorrow.

XXXIII

I had you and I let you go,
never believing in tethers,
certain of your need,
sure that your lies
were camouflage for truth,
unhurt when you strayed,
tolerant of your deceptions.
But shadow had more substance
than the substance of your love.
If they buried ghosts
I would be tossing dirt
on a grave not of my digging.

XXXIV

Time past, I'd display
my spindrift treasures.
But now the cabinets
are sprung and dust mice
play games under the table.
My philosopher's stone
makes lead of our gold.
The royal road
stumbles into bog,
roots catching feet,
spattering mud.

XXXV

There were those days
in which the window
was my frame.
Beyond the reflection
there were houses,
people, moving cars.
On my side was nothing
but the keening phonograph,
the typewriter's rattle,
and in the corner
a stab of light,
a fallen glove.

XXXVI

How very strange to know
that somewhere in this city
you eat and sleep, make love
perhaps a hundred yards away,
that the same water showers us,
the same noises disturb our sleep.
Two thousand miles away
there was more reality to you.

.

XXXVII

The torn flower
lies on the rug.
The unfinished drink
sits on the table
where you left it,
the poems I wrote
beside it, unread.
Standing by the window,
seeing you walk to your car,
I can taste your goodbye.

XXXVIII

You asked me to fashion
truth from a poem
as if a limber line
had some built-in virtue.
But what a poet says is
less truth than poetry.
Only with great luck
could I point out a line
that made a truce with language
and with the anguish
of the anvil speaking
forces a little music.
No poem speaks the truth.
It merely touches a nerve,
scratching conscience.
With you a few lost words
met in darkest Africa,
shook hands, and said,
"A poem, I presume."

XXXIX

No simple thought
could bridge the gap
between my love and yours,
no cardinal's wing
could flush its presence.
Our complex pleasures
foundered in the tide.
What shadow did you see
fixed in the snow,
what menace in my smile?
How simple and unsimple:
We loved enough
to love too much,
no more, no less.

XXXX

I had a dream of you
when we were young.
You had a dream of me
when we were older.
Too bad the dreams
never met.

XXXXI

There was blood
on the knife,
not yours or mine.
You touched it
with your finger.
I tasted it
with my tongue.
It was just blood,
but a beginning.

XXXXII

The words were all wrong.
I said, "Desire."
You said, "Despair."
We changed places,
and it was just the same.

XXXXIII

I knew that you'd come back,
shaking your head or laughing.
There was that destiny
though who could salt it out,
that touch of having been
in all we did together.
Not that the deal was a pat hand,
or that the planets skipped
their courses to make a confluence
for our winter and summer tides.
There was no dovetail to our love.
But our meetings were invested
in a trust and gaiety that parting
anger never washed out, a spark
that danced from pole to pole
easily, with no short circuits.
Then the tide ebbed, the happy ship
lay on its side in puddles on the beach,
a foolish sight, empty of drama.
Metaphor escapes me. The ache
was subcutaneous, a bullet wedged
beneath the skin, thwarting surgery.
It remained, one of a tiny company,
fevering me some nights
when recollection jostled memory,
prodding tenderness and want,
the taste of many days
and the tangents of our love.
It had to be, your coming back,
if only to touch fingertips and run.

XXXXIV

I frightened you—
those were your words—
because I took love
by the scruff
and shook it.
Was your way better
to feed it arsenic
until my nails bled white?

XXXXV

You've said enough goodbyes
to leave an imprint
on my doormat.
What pulls you back
to haunt these hustings?
The pull is not so strong,
your will not weak.
Perhaps you like
the taste of poison.

XXXXVI

It was an old song
in old Spanish,
sprung from the stones
of a dry country.
"My mother bore me
on a dark night.
Nor dog barked,
nor cock crowed."
I sing it now
when there's none
to hear me,
behind a door
that never opens.

XXXXVII

The piecemeal maceration
of my entrails,
unsightly as it is,
must give you satisfaction—
you've been at it so long.

XXXXVIII

There were so many of you,
so few of me.
Yet you took little
when I had much.
But when my store
had dwindled,
you took it all.

XXXXIX

The mind looks at the wine we bought
lying on its side, keeping the cork moist.
The heart finds its own metaphor.
I find your letters in a drawer.
No wine will keep them moist.
The cork has fallen from the bottle.

L

As I walked down the stairs
other presences walked
with me in lockstep—
small rancid dreams,
gestures, the scream
of midnight pity.
Returning I found
the puppets you bought
sitting on chairs,
saying nothing of nothing.

LI

I seldom dream
of real people.
My sleep is inhabited
by ghosts and little men
who giggle.

LII

You at nineteen
warm in the sun,
picking wild strawberries
on a sandy hillside.
You laughing,
wind on your cheeks
in the flurrying snow.
You in wonder,
big with child
soft under my hand.
Everything has died
but this will live
always at high noon.

LIII

There was blood
on my hand
but no hurt
from the gash
that opened to bone.
I put the bucksaw
down and called you.
If I grew faint
it was remembering
that did it, a flash
of other blood and bone
and bandages
tangling the room.

LIV

It was so cold
the rifle barrel
caught my hand
and tore the skin.
Walking guard,
clumsy in layers
of uniform that more
held in the cold
than shut it out,
I thought of fire
and mulling wine.
When I returned
you'd boarded up
the fireplace
and we'd lost
the taste for wine.

LV

I asked: "Why should I
love and lose and love again
with the old love
still festering, pulsing
like an unlanced boil?
Yet I still haul
my bucket of yearning
without any dignity,
like a honeypot,
from door to door."
You asked: "Why try to sing
when you have no voice?"

LVI

Catullus, you've found your boys
and girls and all the rot of Rome
under your nose. You've cut and raped
and chewed both front and back.
You've tasted mouths that reeked
of fish and wine and body parts.
But have you known, Catullus,
the moment when the eyeball bursts
and horses ride across your belly?

LVII

Somewhere on the way
I asked about Heaven.
You smiled
but never answered me.
Heaven was not
a port of call.
But when I spoke
of Hell, you looked
at me with interest.

LVIII

"Try," you said,
"try to break out
before I freeze,
or give me entrance
to your prison."
I might have tried
but it was safe inside.
"Try, please try,"
you said, crying,
shaking the bars.
One movement of my hand
and the walls would crash.
But I knew the peril.

LIX

Standing at the door,
half smile, half frown,
you waved, turned out the light,
and made your exit.
The carpets were too thick
to let me hear your step,
the elevator doors
much too polite to slam.
Yet as my head
filled the hollow
you'd left in the pillow,
I heard the malediction.

LX

It was a simple sunset
for green eyes and blue seas,
but why did you linger on
when the beach sand turned cold.

LXI

Always I've tried
to forge something
in bronze, a kettle
for time past.
But there's no alchemist
to blow on the fire.
You might have been
the artificer.
You might have caught
my hand, guiding
its awkward movement.
The only metal you gave
was pennies for my eyes.

LXII

As I slept you made
a hole in my back,
planting the anodes
of misunderstanding.
When I woke up
you turned the current on.
I felt nothing at all,
but I guess
that was the point.

LXIII

My martyrdom was simple.
There were no nailmarks
on my hands, no blood.
I yawned my morning,
whimpered my evening.
I waited for a sign
to make dirt blossom.
My hand floated in space
to reach you,
to tousle your pity.
When I put my head down,
you were counting angels.

LXIV

Where small things twitch,
gasping their decline,
where bodies float
and fish give immortality,
I left my heart in sedge
for vulture meat.
I left it on a night
too dark, too cold, too wan
for God to happen
on my rejection.
I said, "This muscle
that palpitates but has no hope
will wither like the sedge,
leaving me free,
less damned than when it lived
under a skin that cooked
its own damnation."
It did not die, that heart.
It stretched out on the lake
waiting for hands to renew
its terrible significance.
I took it back, stuffing it
beneath my skin, sheltering it,
though no one cared—not I, not God.

LXV

That was the road we made,
the spoor we left,
from the quiet of the womb
to the stasis of the grave.
That was the chiaroscuro
of our anonymous features,
the antiphonal clusters
making our birthsong
and our requiem.
The child stares at ants,
Old men watch grasshoppers.
To question it casts
dead fish in the ocean.
Amplify the cry at birth,
the grunt at orgasm,
the wheeze as death
deflates the carcass.
Did it mean more to Adam,
to Milton blind,
or to the driver bleeding
slowly on the highway?

LXVI

I saw it once,
the image of myself
floating out of reach
among the tree leaves.
But how could I,
planted on earth,
see my image float
when face down
in the snow
I was carved
in heavy ice?
If you can tell me
I will take your hand
and put it
to these lips.
I'll see myself
and pierce your tears.

LXVII

The red shutters have been painted
grey in the house we lived in.
There are heavy drapes on the windows
where light burst out all night.
But the trees remain, in the autumn
shedding leaves like a monster snowfall.
The little dogwood, just a stalk
when I spared it must have flowered
by now, dropping its petals in spring.
I never pass the place that held us,
but I remember its many shelters,
the bedroom fireplace glowing
and bursting its resined wood
that I cut in anger or affection.
Now we are gone, the continuity broken.
The children are gone and think of us
only to tease nostalgia on dull nights.
Now we trudge in the long apathy
between the joy and the bother,
living between other people's walls,
the broken china of tomorrow's middens.

LXVIII

I ask it, not pressing for response,
but ask it still, hoping that your answer
will quiet the pounding of the hammers.
Where, on what beach, what battlefield,
did we engage our troops, where look
on Carthage like a dream warm-rinsed
and rising to the sun, where clasp
our eyes or tear away the sackcloth?
In the rich gore of your triumph
you did not strike me, squelch my mouth,
or crunch my testicles.
You did not offer pity or demand mine
as men victorious comfort their repentance.
But why, when wind and spit gagged
at my insolence, did you reach out
and touch my angry tears and smile?

LXIX

You will in time discern
that the farther wall recedes,
returning when you blink your eyes.
Small objects in the room change places,
appear and disappear into the ceiling.
Far away there is a honking
as of geese or of men dying.
And little men invest the corners,
lying in wait until you doze
before cracking their knuckles.

LXX

Stand not on the order
of your going, my lords.
Make for the exit, run
from this bleeding thing,
this effigy of a man
who asks no pity of you,
prays only for your silence
as he snorts and groans
his final statement.
Throw open the doors
and leave his pleadings
disemboweled on the rug.
Death is the meter,
not your scurrying footsteps.
He will in time
be bound over to the arbiters
of all mortality,
the caretakers of flesh,
the tender crawlers
who wait to celebrate
his new virginity.

LXXI

Persephone, you know
too well men's fear of death
to joke with me.
I paid my penny,
rode the ferry here.
spirit without flesh,
yet tingling at the toes
and fingers, not yet
experienced in the etiquette
of death. I watched
the rising shapes of Hell
but never saw the fires.
I listened for the cries
of baking souls,
heard only music.
You called out once
to me or someone else.
I heard the call
but saw only mist.
I struggled to assume
some form
so you would know me
or show yourself.
But the streets of Hell
are neither hot nor cold—
just empty.

LXXII

The wafer and the wine are sacraments
of personal flesh and wine.
We eat ourselves and find no nourishment.
The theme from womb to tomb
is phrased in sound beyond notation,
known but never caught in symphony.
The unvoiced music dies in our ears.
We are torn from our genesis
and left to dry on an empty beach,
reaching up for God but inwardly
recoiling from his touch.

These poems, Jacques Barzun wrote to Ralph de Toledano, are notable for "the perfect ease with which your individual tongue speaks. There are no borrowed fluencies, and it all sounds as if there were no other way to put the case."

Stripping language and poetic expression to the bare essentials, Toledano's poems are almost conversational, in the Catullan mode. Yet rarely does a poet explore the love/hate relationship of men and women with the intensity and depth of *Poems: You & I.*

This, Toledano's eighteenth book and first published collection of verse, represents a journey which ventures into the bright and darker sides of the human condition. The brilliant imagery of his poetic sensibility and recall is set against an ironic view of love as "a field where many die but few find resurrection."

The *you* to whom the poems are addressed, like the *I*, is both one and many,